JOURNEY

THE MOSES EXPERIENCE

PROJECT

Awakening of Leadership

Identity Release

Free to Free Others

MEGAN J.

Holy Spirit Inspired

ISBN 978-1-0980-7590-3 (paperback)
ISBN 978-1-63903-861-9 (hardcover)
ISBN 978-1-0980-7591-0 (digital)

Christian Faith Publishing, Inc.
832 Park Avenue
Meadville, PA 16335
www.christianfaithpublishing.com

Cover Design by: Gloria Kober

Printed in the United States of America

DEDICATION

To GOD, be all the Glory! As I am thankful unto him for speaking to my heart concerning different experience's we can have in our life time, and the fact that we can refer to the "*Holy Bible*" for examples instructions & insight that can be applied to our lives on a daily basis.

"In order to relate to someone or something there must be a common ground or thread." in that there is a connection that can speak louder than words could ever say.

I would like to in remembrance and dedication to the late "Evangelist Ella K Johnson" my Mother, who was my first example of who God is through her life and experience's she had, And how she was able to through much study and teaching of scriptures lives and instilled that form of love in my heart, that in-spite of life's adversities there is an answer there is a remedy and certainty there is a solution wrapped up in the Gospel message of life hope and liberty for all those who seek and search for it with their whole heart and mind!

Megan J

Contents

ACKNOWLEDGMENT

To all the spiritual Leaders Ministers Pastors & lay-members of the body of Christ and to my family & friends that have spoken into my life words of encouragement as well as correction. Thank—you!

For without both there is no growth!

Just like the balancing of the Word of God & Faith is a must for *EVERY* Believer!

—Megan J

PREFACE

TO THE READER:

I want you to take a walk with me through the pages of this book, maybe you have read the story line about the persons in which we will talk about. It's *OK* if you have, I want you to take a closer look through the eyes of another—Me! Then see what you see for yourself as it unfolds for you to see even more.

This is what God has given me for You!

Especially for those He is calling from the drama & trauma life has brought and the lost thing's which happened because of being chosen for greatness that may be hidden from you right now, by what has happened to you in the past or present or in the life of someone you may know, You will be able to direct them with a different perspective that can be transforming and a lasting change.

You may be hidden in plain view; you may be young or older just know there is something radical about the thing's God has planned with you in mind like in the life of Moses.

So whatever the experience you have had in life with life and throughout your life there is a beginning a midway season and an end, A conclusion to it all, let it be unto you according to Gods will and Gods way!

"Luke 1:37 ~ Be it unto me according to thy word"

INTRODUCTION

The Moses Experience is about experiencing God for yourself and the different places and stages that you may find yourself in life from not knowing who you really are to isolating and a new beginning which opens up and sets the stage to meet the originator of life itself, God!

Take a look, take a glance, and take time to read and reread with you in mind. Where are you going? What really is in store for you? Will you settle with the deep personal relationship with God and do his bidding, or would you rather enjoy the pleasures of this world and in the end be in eternal loss and hopelessness.

Though Moses didn't receive the benefit of the Promised Land, he received the better part of a life looked at because of humility and obedience to the purpose in which he was called and chosen for.

He was a part of the plan and the purpose which God proved himself to the people he choose to reveal himself to. And the fact that man cannot live by *bread* alone but by every word that proceeds out of the mouth of God (Deuteronomy 8:3, Matthew 4:1–4).

Do you know what it feels like to be a sore thumb? To not quite fit in or maybe seeing things differently than others?

Well, you may be experiencing something others may have felt at one point or time in their lives. Is it an experience? Is it a journey? Or is it just a part of your life? You have to obtain what is needed to get through it, to know it, to understand it, but mainly to *accept it* and in it be made free!

This book serves as a manual and a guide into the life of a man from birth who felt and experienced, then became a witness of a lifelong journey of change, challenges, and ultimately victory that would affect him and impact the lives of a whole nation of people and still echoing in the time we now live in.

The name *Moses* comes from the Hebrew verb, meaning "to pull out/draw out." "To be drawn out" was an incredibly significant part of who he was and a real experience he had at birth. God drawing him out to draw him into a life that would one day change him as he would become one of the greatest men whom God chose to record by way of writing the first *law* of God, the structure that was laid out for mankind to live by, and a foundation of Faith to know God in a more real and intimate way!

My question to you, "What is God drawing you out of? Or out of you? And to what where or whom is he sending you?" As a *voice*, a *messenger*, or maybe even a *deliverer* to those who are waiting for you to be born and take your rightful place in God and in his kingdom here on earth!

Megan. S. Johnson
Servant of the Lord Jesus Christ.

Who Am I?

First, *you* come to a place where this question is directed to you. This is before starting anything in life, knowing who you are and what part you play in whatever it is you plan to do, where you are and where you are coming from are factors that must be addressed.

Then to the *one* who has formed, created, called, and chosen you for the destiny that awaits in the knowing of *self* and having a sense of real purpose, confidence, and reality that will sure you up for the task.

This is also the question Moses posed to God (Exodus 3:11).

And Moses, when he was called upon to go as a voice and a messenger to Pharaoh, told him to "*let my people go*" (Exodus 9:1), people who were at that time in bondage and slavery, which he would become the *deliverer* to in spite of at one time being next in line as a Pharaoh and raised as an Egyptian. Who was he really? It had to be revealed in time and was connected to what he was sent by God to do, *be* the guide to the way of escape to the Promised Land (place). It was Moses, the leader of *God's* choice!

It starts with *God* and you. Sometimes we all question ourselves as to "who am I?" that I should this or that, or even the other bottom line, why not you or me? Why?

The questioning of self...*why?* To come to some conclusions and answers that will make a difference, give direction, and sometimes new life, hope, and dreams; to also make bold steps and strides in the process of life and time; and most of all, to know who you are and the fact that *you* matter. You are the answer to someone's prayer, you are the key to someone's door, and to deliverance, you were created for this!

Note: *Moses wrote the first five books of the Bible.*

Chapter 1

The Question Who Am I?

As we look into the book of Genesis 1:27, we see a vivid account and picture drawn out for us to view as the *beginning and blueprint* of the world and mankind.

So "God created man in his own image, in the image of God created he him; male and female created he them" (Genesis 1:27).

You have a creator as you have a beginning. That is a good place to start when asking yourself, "Who am I?" Your answer: you are a created being in the image and the likeness of someone...God.

You are made up of *three distant parts/components.*

1. *Your physical part* (which makes you world consciousness)
   To exist on the earth, you need a *body.*
2. *Your soulish part* (which makes you *self*-consciousness)
   This is your heart/mind/will, the seat/core of your *emotions*, the part that gives you an awareness of *who you are* and your personality!
3. *Your spirit part* (which makes you alive and is intricately connected to your *soul*)
   This is the part of you that becomes *born again* and spiritually alive when you are reconnected to God *through Jesus Christ* who has created you!

Your life experience has the ability to shape you into who you decide to be and become, sometimes positive and sometimes negative. Without good and proper guidance/leadership and a perfectly balance wheel, it can be hard to grasp, let alone hold onto as a navigation through the dark times you may and often will face in life.

The soul part of our being is like an incubator; it takes in and germinates (grows) like a yielding of a harvest it holds onto, then produce. What? What we have *seen, heard, and felt are all part of our God-given senses.*

It also factors in how we respond or react to situations in life as our minds process the "who, what, when, and where" that has happened to us.

Important fact: As born-again believers of the Lord Jesus Christ and as you take the steps for true identity, learn, understand, know, and practice daily the principles that are the instructions in the Bible on a *godly charterer* (Hebrew 5:8–9) that has the power and ability to change *you*, who you are, where you have been, and a better determination to where you *are* going!

Let us look at "who am I" a little closer from the perspective and vantage point of where you may have been.

Moses learned the ways and practices of Egyptians, a type of the world *living* outside of the acknowledgment of *God* (creator) and originator of life. He wasn't aware of the bloodline that he really had. He was taught how to rule with an iron fist, yet it did not shape him to be that way or with a hard heart toward those less fortune and those who suffer. Why? Because the one who purposed his being placed something inside of him that would one day come to the forefront of who he was, but did that make him perfect? *No*. He struggled with an identity crisis and anger, especially when something or someone wasn't right.

God has a way of taking the things that are bad, even weaknesses, and turning it around for the good, for change, and for his glory, especially when you submit yourself to him.

The Mirror Is Always Reflecting

Have you ever looked into the mirror, and it's not liked what you've seen, not because your hair wasn't done, or your cut wasn't fresh, but something inside did not feel right or good.

What did you do? How did/do you deal with you? Do you constantly say or think negative thoughts about yourself or putting yourself down? Why? When did it start? And where did it come from?

It didn't come from you but from a source or someone. Where then?

In focusing on "Who am I," it's also necessary to take those moments to *stop* and recognize that something is wrong, something is a little off, and it must be put back on track. Being aware of that is a good thing. Just don't allow yourself to linger there too long.

Self-awareness is good in a sense that you aren't oblivious of who you are. Do *not* become your own enemy!

No matter what and how terrible of a thing that has or will happen in your life, it doesn't define *you*. It just happened to happen to you! You have the God-given ability to walk in *freedom* or condemnation (Romans 8:1), especially when you have made the *choice* to walk with God and live your life with him in the driver's seat. You are sure to reach the appointments that he has set for your life!

Changing the inside is a specialty of a savior (Jesus). There are people you must save by way of leading them to the other side of through as Moses did, so as you get out of your own way with *self-doubt* and fear, you can be the person that you were meant to be in answering the question.

I am who God said I am. *Period!*

Find every scripture in the Holy Bible that gives you your new identity and take it to heart every promise of God. Be a reflection of a better image of yourself through a renewed *mind*, not a shattered, distorted mirror that will keep you looking back in despair and hopelessness!

To end this *chapter*, here are a few *points to ponder and words to embrace.*

What is God *drawing out of you* that you will know who you are as an individual?

What is God *drawing or pulling you out of that* you will know him? Hear his voice clearly and *seek him* more and more until you can fully understand.

What is it? Who you are in God, in life, and in this world?

What is GOD *drawing you into or to do?*

Have you settled it in your mind and in your heart to surrender *all* and take it one day and one step at a time?

Will you believe and trust that *you can do it*?

He is with you. He has and will equip you in matters of who you are.

How can a rocky or rough life with a harsh beginning be turned around in such a way that if you had to let go of everything that you have and feel you've gained will be the truce and turning point of a profound life that will be of God's choosing?

The I Am sent me!

God turning it around for Moses and his question with the answer for you and I that the "I AM" that dwells in us loves us, chooses us, and can be seen with clarity of knowledge and understanding that we can stand with confidence of words and speech, so instead of *who am I*, it's *I am* because you are *God*!

Be reminded that this is the *day* that the Lord has made.

Declare to yourself *daily*, "I will rejoice and be glad in it" (Psalms 118:24).

Some names of God in the Old Testament scriptures for reference (*from the Hebrew and Greek translation*).

- *El Shaddai (Lord God Almighty)*
- *El Elyon (The Most High God)*
- *Adonai (Lord, Master)*
- *Yahweh (Lord, Jehovah)*
- *Jehovah Nissi (The Lord My Banner)*
- *Jehovah Raah (The Lord My Shepherd)*
- *Jehovah Rapha (The Lord That Heals)*
- *Jehovah Shammah (The Lord Is There)*

- *Jehovah Tsidkenu (The Lord Our Righteousness)*
- *Jehovah Mekoddishkem (The Lord Who Sanctifies You)*
- *El Olam (The Everlasting God)*
- *Jehovah Jireh (The Lord Will Provide)*
- *Jehovah Shalom (The Lord Is Peace)*
- *Jehovah Sabaoth (The Lord of Hosts)*

In the Old Testament times, a *name* was not only identification but was *an identity* as well. Many times, a special meaning was attached to the name. Names also had other purposes as an explanatory purpose.

Throughout Scripture, *God* reveals himself to us through his names. When we study these names that he reveals to us in the Bible, we can get a better understanding of who *God really is*. The meanings behind *God's names* reveal the central personality and nature of the one who bears them.

Read through the names and see God working and moving throughout and in your life as the meaning of the name will become more and more evident to you!

And remember whose you are. You were created by an almighty and awesome God that loves you just like you are but loves you too much to leave you the way you *are*! Change is growth, the *I am* in you.

Who am I?

- *The Question?*
- *The answer!*
- *Who am I created in the image and likeness of?*
- *How can my life and story be related to that of Moses?*
- *For what have I been called and chosen to be a deliverer of?*
- *How can I use my wound/scars to help heal someone else?*
- *And in what way?*
- *What lesson can I take away from the life of Moses in the beginning of his journey?*

- *What questions do I have that only God can show me the answers to?*
- *What can I add to make this chapter more personal/real to me and others?*

Chapter 2

The Call
True Identity

David *Shelly* *Mary* *Beth* *Karen*
Michael *William* *Leslie* *Frank* *Margaret*
Samuel *Lisa* *Amanda* *Mark* *John* *Lori* *Lois* *Richard*

Did you read all those names? Do you get the picture? It is as though you are calling those people by name!

It is as if God himself is calling your name, and *he* is!

There are different types of *calls* and different *times* of a call. But know this *you are called* by God to your identity. It does not matter where you are right now, what you are into, or what you are doing, God has a way of calling you by dealing with your soul and spirit. That part of you that you can't get away from, you will begin to wonder about things that you may have forgotten or haven't thought about in a long time like life, death, and eternity. Is it all real? Who is God? Why is the world the way it is? Then it will all take on a whole new meaning to you as it is revealed. You will feel a sense of urgency for spiritual things and people like going on a retreat in search of things that are of significance. There are many different ways in which you can be drawn into a reality that there is more than what you see, and it is time for more!

To those who have answered the first *call* of salvation, he is still calling you into deeper levels and places of his Spirit that will usher you into the greatness he has for you, which is him in you doing his will.

When *Moses* had to leave Egypt not by choice but by force (Exodus 2:11–15), he found himself far from what he knew what he was used to and in an unfamiliar place with unfamiliar people. He had to start from the bottom where he was used to always being on top looking down. But according to scripture not high-minded or ruthless toward those who did not have and those who suffered like the slaves who were bound in Egypt or the women he met at the well (Exodus 2:16–17).

When life takes uncertain turns and those turns leave you somewhere else or somewhere you have never been before, especially when it is out of your control, there is something *called a God moment.* Those are the times you will begin to see the working of the hand and direction of God in your life. It may seem like the world has fallen around you. *Take heart and faith*, there is more in store for you. Begin to look for new ways, new open doors, and new avenues that may be the threshold of stepping out of life and living a certain way and into living life for a higher purpose and cause. *It may just be your call* to what has been buried inside of you, your *true identity*!

Moses road to the *high place*, which literally was a mountain (Horeb), where *God's spirit dwelled.* It was in that land where he found himself alone, working away from his known place of birth and upbringing. All he knew was that he was open and ready to hear and see something that was so amazing that it would change him and his life forever (Exodus 3:1–3).

Midian…

Where is your (Midian) high place? The place where you will meet God. Have you gotten there? Where is it located? The place where God has drawn you to see his glory, the very manifested expression of his power, for it is in that place where the real you can come out and be cleansed from all that is in you and be made whole and humbled. You will hear and see the *call of God* as he ushers you into himself, to be made known of him, his existence, his love, his grace, and yes, his consumption of fire, which represents purity. Anything that is used in which we eat from like a utensil or instrument, it must *first* go through a purifying system and process. God's presence sometimes like a *consuming fire* will burn off and burn away every evil or demonic force from you and from your life!

And as he commune/talk with you *Spirit to spirit*, you will do as Moses did, "Bow down, obey, and let go, take off anything that can't exist in the presence of God and you will answer the call by saying" (Exodus 3:4–5).

Here am I, which in turn means "Yes, I am here. Speak, Lord!"

Who could resist? Who can deny such an experience like this! An experience that will change and set the course of life to bring you into the place and purposed destiny.

God.

The very *one* who spoke, and it was he who requested you in *his* presence to have a conversation with you, to explain things to you, to give you a different perspective about yourself, where you came from, and the fact he has chosen you for a journey in which he plans to be bigger than life to people who are bound (*The Children of Israel for Moses*). Who are for you?

We see in scripture the people he was sent to were not always so grateful and so patient of people (Exodus 16:2, Numbers 14:2).

But we see he had an everlasting love for them as he has for you and me (Jeremiah 31:3, 1 John 4:9–11).

And to those who in return will love him (Deuteronomy 7:9).

Moses, taking off his shoes, is like a representation of taking off the old and walking into the new, the holy place of God!

Are you willing? Are you willing to go? Are you willing to take off what is required of you? And do as he did? Are you willing to set aside anger or misfortune and take up the call of the one who called you? Can you identify with Moses and those who are *caught* in between where they were, where they are, and where they are going? *Translation*: place of change from one to another, one bad situation to what may look like or seem, yet another will you find yourself willing and open to the realm of the Spirit of a holy, merciful, and loving but of consuming-*fire* God (Hebrews 12:29–29).

What has happened in your life that has caused you to run, leave, or escape from one place to somewhere else like Moses? Was it your own doing? Does it have the potential to bring you right where you need to be for something greater to be revealed to you as your *true identity* from God and his way of putting the missing pieces together of your life so you can better understand you, your life and your journey?

Is it in incarceration, prison, or jail? Is it in the basement of your parents' house? Maybe a relationship that has gone bad, and you don't know which way to go? A lonely and a foreign place? Wherever you may find yourself, *stop* and let God find you! As he is calling you by name and in your current circumstance, let it become the high place where you meet God!

As God revealed himself to Moses in Exodus 3:6, it took him by storm. Sure, he had questions about his real father and family. Surely he was buzzing around about his true identity and how the Pharaoh's daughter found him and raised him as her own. That must have been an awful feeling inside, but here was God, filling in the blanks of his life story, and at a time, he had nothing but what lay ahead of him. As God spoke things to him, he became afraid and hid his face. The awesomeness of the one who knows it all, the why and the what.

I can image it was a wow moment in the life of Moses. Here he was seeing a bush in the desert burning but not up, and then a *voice* spoke, not only talking but giving instructions and information that would cause him to go back to a place he knew but as a different person entirely.

At that moment, none of it mattered. He was at a low-enough place that he was in need of the miraculous, and God was the one to give it to him. It was all that was needed to tie up all the questions, concerns, and confusions he had faced. Now he could have a clean slate because of his creator and begin life all over again with the knowledge and experience that he had and what would be a help to the people he was about to become a leader to.

To end *chapter 2*, here are a few *points to ponder with questions and answers to embrace.*

- *Have I met with God?*
- *Have I accepted the fact that God has called me?*
- *If yes, explain how I know.*
- *Has the call revealed my identity?*
- *In what ways?*
- *What experiences have I had that now I can see it as a high place where I met with God?*
- *What experiences have I had that has shaped my life?*
- *In what way?*
- *After looking at the life of Moses, how can I apply these things to my life and how can it also help in the lives of others?*
- *Am I willing to answer the call and walk it out as God sees fit for my life?*
- *What is the call?*
- *How do I know?*

Chapter 3

THE QUEST
ARE YOU UP FOR THE JOURNEY?

Are you up for the journey?

It's wonderful when you decide to go on a trip maybe with some friends or some family. You plan, prepare, and perhaps get a map of some sort or use the handy GPS. However, you choose to travel. Are up for the distance, long or short? Maybe there are delays or road-blocks. How is the weather? And how will it be during your drive, flight, train, or bus ride? All of this can be a no-brainer. When you have done this before, maybe you are going to a familiar place, or you did your part in *planning ahead*. It can be pleasant in its prepping for it, especially when *you* made it up in your mind to go! You're a little more up for the journey and maybe looking forward to it. What happens when it turns into a quest? Environmental changes and unforeseen difficulties can make you not as up for it than usual. What if it's a trip you really didn't want to take but had to?

In life, we make a lot of decisions to go places. Some of them are good, and some of them are not as good as we would like, but we make the decision.

What happens when you are called upon to stand in for someone and do a task that you aren't as comfortable as you would be because it's out of your normal range or place that you are familiar with? Will you still go? Will you still do it?

It boils down to are you up for the journey even if it becomes a quest? It boils down to will you make the decision?

Time

Time is a factor in traveling.
Time is a factor in preparing.
Time is a factor in waiting!

Yes, *time* is a factor in knowing God and in you getting to the places he has for you to go!

This stands true in a spiritual journey with God. There are days and times in walking with God, living from day to day, that the feelings of being out of sort will come, not sure if you are heading in the right direction in your learning and pursuing him with all you have, let alone taking the right vehicle to get you there. Are you *praying* in a manner that leads you into a deep and meaningful conversation with God that when you are done *praying*, you feel that relief that he heard you, and you are sure that you have heard from him?

In these times and situations, you must reach further than yourself, what you see and what you feel, as if you are searching for a place that you are going regardless of the surrounding circumstances, what's going on, and what may be getting in your way, like traveling on a road you have never been on before.

Faith (*believing*) in him can be utilized in this way to be your guide.

That is what testimonies are made from; there was a test you survived. Why? You didn't give up; you held on; you went beyond the surface and allowed something higher in.

An almighty God will invade a situation in your life that may have brought despair and confusion. In spite of it, there is a calm in the midst of it because you decided to focus on what is necessary and continue on, and in it, there comes a peace and a comfort that you are not alone. Even if physically you are, God's spirit is with you!

What does it take to be mentally ready for life's journey?

Will you be in agreement to what it involves? What will it take to get you from one point to the next? And what are the most important factors of it all?

Time plays an important role not only in your birthing and in the realization of who you are all the way to the place where God steps out of nowhere and begins to speak volumes to your life. Also, the moments, minutes, seconds, hours, days, weeks, and years that it will take to life a full and complete life with Creator God on the inside of you!

As God is God, he will give victory to those who will trust in him. Though you may feel afraid and unsure, he will give you strength from on high as he did his people in Old Testament times and still today! It is recorded for us to know God, the Greatest Warrior, and will cause you to win *Psalms 83*. As you read, you will see that the *high place* can be something for one but something different for another. There were enemies in *Midian* that sought to fight against *the children of Israel (the people of God)*.

But God, who hears, sees, and knows *all*, is a defense against your enemies! Be encouraged in knowing when you stand for God. He will stand for you when you *fight* for God. He will fight for you! How? By *you* holding on, by *you* believing, and by *you* not giving in to circumstances that will take you in a different direction and away from him. Who he is is what *he* stands for and what he requires of you. We see God fighting for his people in *Scripture*. We can also see God fighting for *believers* today!

Will you allow God's time to heal what is broken in you? So the change can be made in you? Can you see Moses going from riches to literally rags? Do you think he needed some time to deal with it and accept the *sudden* changes in his life and truly accept his new one? Will you to be victorious as God begins to make the needed cuts of bonds that you have grown accustomed to? What does that feel like? Is it an easy transition? It may not be. I would say *no*, it is not!

The consolation is when there is a humbling of *self* and the decision to accomplish the quest realizing in it there will be danger, delays, and maybe some destruction to see, feel, and handle like a *long-term relationship* with someone. Once you really have been to the mountain of God, *the high place*, you will understand, even as you have taken off the *old*, what you had, what was yours, and you *willingly* laid it down to now step into God, who he is, what he is about, and what you will learn of him. You made a *quantum leap* into the unknown, and it's okay! The promises of God are *sure* as he is (1 Corinthians 1:20). You just have to be the one to *stay* the course on the road, in the direction, through the difficulties the down, and seemingly, out times to see him as he unveils himself to you and those in which you are assigned and sent to.

Buckle up spiritually!

Are you *up* for the *time challenge*?

Are you up for what it's going to take as time is factored in while coming into alignment with the God of your journey? All it will be for the quest that you will travel in is your obedience to him and what he has planned.

With time being an element to consider, it can be an enemy, or you can allow it to be a friend. You choose! Make the decision on a regular and daily basis as you travel on the road that will lead you to where you are supposed to be and the road that you will lead others on as well.

You will find that God is not in a hurry, nor will he speed up time for you when there are intricate details he wants you to get, parts of information that must be clear, as well as followed. It's like he takes you on a winding road as he will be the guide so you can learn his voice, know his ways, how to walk with him, and walk out what lies ahead of you. Learn how to trust him and ultimately learn how to love and obey Him more and more and more. It never ends as long as *you* are up for the *quest and journey*. It will be just that, a continuous progression of time and space with you and your creator!

It may feel like all the searching is rigorous, the ins and the outs, but we can look at Moses and see how God allowed him *time*. It took *forty years on the backside of the desert* for him to be ready to accomplish the plan of God. Why? Because it takes time! Everyone because of their own distinct makeup and personalities will be on a time frame that determines God's time frame for their lives. Remember God is not in a hurry, so don't you be! *But* the sooner you submit to him, the sooner you will see the moving of his spirit as he moves you to where he is calling and sending you.

It was forty *years* that the children of Israel wondered in the wilderness. Why? Was disobedience a factor for them? Or was it a matter of a willingness to totally surrender to God so they could walk in full obedience to him and what he required of them to do.?

However long it takes for you to see God and not your problems, his glory and not your desire to stay in a place where you are passing through, a state of guessing and wondering around but seeing what God wants you to see, he is willing to wait for you. We see it in scripture. Because of the lack of faith and trust though, he had already delivered them out of Egypt, yet they still choose to doubt. Was it because they would rather rely on something else rather than him? They believed the people's report rather than remembering how God had already preformed miracles for them. They choose to believe they were like grasshoppers. To the inhabitants of the land and believed that the people were giants compared to them. God waited until the doubters were deceased, and the hearts and the minds of them that were left were ready to take what rightfully belonged to them.

He blessed them to go in and possess the land. It was all a matter of time, a matter of the quest being a part of the journey!

Will you rely on something that has the potential but will fail or on something that has been tried and true? Will it take a lifetime to submit and surrender? Or will you take the real steps of faith and take him at his word and proven power to save heal deliver and accomplish what he has said he will do.

With time not always on your side, you can make it a friend. How? By letting it work for you and *you* not against it! Such as, what time is it? What is it time for? What is the particular thing you can be gaining and growing in? Is it wisdom? Is it knowledge of yourself, God, the enemies of God, and this world we live in?

Time can better equip you like a road trip, where you have packed, what you may need in case of an emergency that would arise *you literally* took the time to do something that may be vital to you and make you better prepared, what time and experience will do for you when viewed right can be a friend to you if you allow it!

Surely, Moses learned patience, mercy, and grace. He experienced it himself on his road to meeting God. Losing what he had, he would find himself gaining something more tangible and real as a relationship with the one who started it all.

God took time to tell him by way of showing himself to him in the high place. After God let him wait, he was ready and open to the ultimate journey and quest to speak on the behalf of *God*, something that was not of human doing or perception or a choice to believe but of the awesome manifesting power of himself to those he choose to speak to!

Moses talked to God *face-to-face*, and it was evident and very clear to the inhabitants of the land. Moses did not look the same, feel the same, think, talk, or act the same. Why? Because he had been in the presence of *El Elyon, the Most High God!*

Wow! What an honor! After journeying and finding something or someone that you weren't really looking for and to be a guest in their presence, even if at first, you didn't even know you were looking or longing for it, but because it was time for the glorious encounter, it happened!

What response will you have *in that* face-to-face? Will it then be *worth it to you*? Will it not be an honor that was worth the trip?

End of chapter 3.

Reflection and Review

- *Am I up* for the journey?
- In what way can I say I am?
- Do I know what the journey is?
- In what ways can I better prepare for it
    1. spiritually,
    2. mentally,
    3. emotionally, and
    4. physically?
- Is the quest the same as the journey?
- What is the difference?
- What life experiences can I say has prepared me for the quest?

- What are some time factors I can embrace?
- What are some time factors I need to eliminate?
- What things can I see in Moses's life that I can see in my life?

When Moses went back to Egypt, he was a *changed man*! He was no longer the young prince of Egypt; he was now the *servant* of the *Lord God*. He must now face the enemy without! In him, facing the enemy within (himself). And in his facing God, he was ready for next and more. The turning point of *change* in his life and the encounter alone was enough, now the outcome and his acceptance of the call was to go save the people in which he once was a part of ruling over.

No one could have impacted his life in that manner that would make him consider facing a place and a people that had become an enemy to him.

Pause at the thought of *the change to deal with the real enemy*. What an entrance! What an eye-opener! It's the wonderful feeling that you can have because the change has taken place in your heart, mind, body, soul, and spirit.

Now the change must be followed by action and not just any action but a direct hit to the walls of a known enemy. It's just like God change you to be a light of change to those in which you will need the testimony and power of his greatness firsthand.

We all know and are aware that there is a *real enemy*, once he was an angel, now cast out and downed by God and known to the people who are on the earth. There was change that happened with him as well, one that you do not want to be a victim or a prey of! *Pride!*

The cause of Lucifer desiring to "be like the most high God" (Isaiah 14:12–17).

Pride is a feeling or deep pleasure or satisfaction derived from "one's own" achievements of those with whom one is closely associated or from qualities or possessions that are widely admired.

Chapter 4

The Change
Dealing with the Real Enemy!

After you have come toe to toe with *you* and you have been beaten by *truth*, you welcome change! The kind of change that is much needed and necessary to go on in life being who you were born to be with the acceptance of *self*. One that even people around you can see and say, "Wow, you have changed!" Let's step in the arena of life and say you find yourself being under the scrutiny of people concerning the same things all the time or even most of the time, let alone *some of the time*.

You find yourself falling into the same trip or trap that you did a year ago or even longer. Wouldn't you say it's a matter of *changing* your view and perception so you can see the snowball coming and get out of its way. Why? Because you have changed, yes, you can even say you have grown. Maturity has been the result of long hard battles you have had to fight and overcome. It now is welcomed by you, so you do not have to feel the heat or the wrath that comes from failing to do things right, better, or different.

You can be the gladiator in the arena with hands upheld because the victory was in your surrender to the only one that has the means to bring you to the point of change and help you make the transition into being victorious in matters of your own heart and life. Sometimes it's not easy, and some moments can be painful, but knowing the purpose and outcome that it is *all* working together for your good can ease the most troubled mind (Romans 8:28).

Well, that's done. That phase has concluded with all of its wonder, and there remains a *servant* waiting for the commands to carry out in the most humbled and obedient way that will yield in the gratification that the reward is yet to come of the Lord!

Change is never easy, but it's worth it all in the end!

Without it, there would be no growth, no new discoveries, and no new paths to chart though God never changes (Malachi 3:6). He does new things (Isaiah 43:19). Even the flowers that bloom in its new season aren't the same as the flowers from the year before. They are new ones, same in type and touch but new to the human eyes to behold and wonderful. After a long cold winter, to smell the fragrance of fresh flowers can bring a delight to the senses even of those who may not like or even be a lover of them!

When you have the raw material of some kind, there is a process that it must go through in order for change to occur like jewels, fine glass, or china to bring out the best and make it into something different. Like clay, the potter must determine what things must be done to have a complete and finished work!

Whatever the thing may be or become, it can't refuse, or shall I say the power is in the hands of who holds the thing. Such is the same with you and I. God who had you in his mind since the beginning of time (Jeremiah 1:5) shows you. He knew you, and he knew what it would take to bring you to this present moment in your life for you to not only be in search of change but to embrace it with a knowledge and understanding that it is good. He is at the pivotal point of it all. He knows the steps it would take for you to be at the end of the road with change in view. He would make sure that you choose life (Deuteronomy 30:19), which means choose the life of change that will give you everlasting life, a life pleasing unto him. He has provided this by way of *Jesus Christ* (Acts 4:12). In your acceptance of this, you will be made spiritually alive, born again, reconnected to God the Father who by way of his *Holy Spirit* will be with and in you, birthing change one spiritual step at a time.

You will be able to navigate and deal with anything that will come to take you back into a life, place, or state of mind that is anything less than what God has said or have done for you!

Moses changed, and Moses was set to change others by his experience and by what he did as one who was delivered will now be a deliverer to many people! A whole group of people who became a nation. God talked a long time with Moses. He took him back to the beginning of time, gave him records and accounts of the lives of significant people who because of them we have the spiritual birthright and promises of God.

Now that is a change worth fighting for. That is a change worth envisioning! God raising up people who will not bow down to those who have set themselves against him.

Who is an Enemy? Any opposing force to what God says and what God has established as so. What is an enemy? Anything that has formed itself against you (Romans 8:31).

In dealing with an enemy, you must be aware that there is one, and not be sidetracked into thinking or believing that it does not exist.

When God told Moses to tell Pharaoh, "Let my people go," he also told him he would hardened his heart, that he would not obey (Exodus 9:12). Why? For reasons that would prove his greatness, and that he loved them enough to *save* them, and they to needed change. What a display of their exiting, an *Exodus, a mass departure of people, withdrawal, leaving, escape, fleeing.*

God dealt harshly with the Egyptians in the process of delivering his people out that should have turned their hearts fully toward God. For some, it did not. For some, it did. They received the Promised Land (Genesis 26:3, Deuteronomy 26:7–9). It is amazing to see the great lengths God will go to deal with our enemies and us. Don't let things move you away from doing what he has chosen for you to do because it's not what you like or desire to do. Someone is counting on you to speak and fight on their behalf!

Everyone will not celebrate the new person you have become; they may not consider it a good thing that has happened to you. They may even criticize you saying that you are not as good as a person you used to be, and that they don't like the person you have become. *Beware!* This sounds like the voice of the enemy casting doubt and fear on the decision you have made.

This is not strange to a follower of God, nor should it be for someone who has just been spiritually awakened to the things of God. People will size up for what it should look like, not realizing that your blueprint comes from the Lord daily. You seek it out in every situation life brings.

Thankfully the laid out instructions show and strengthen you in the great change that has occurred through the lives of people to read about that can help shape you as the potter has you on his wheel as those who we know are in our lives. Watch out for the hidden agenda of the *real enemy* who goes about seeking who he may devour (1 Peter 5:8).

And the enemy that you will be sent back to face on your job, at home, school, or who you are married to. Dealing with it, God's way is always the best way.

Even if at first, it appears there is no *change with them* and them hearing you is not in sight, whatever God's plan is it will be his expected outcome. Embrace the part you play in the picture. *Let God be God* and you his servant!

How do you know if he isn't getting their attention through you and the fact you are a witness to the presence of his ability for *change*? It can also be God's way of saving you from them that one day, he can in turn save them too!

It's also not something you should fight or hold onto deal with yes, but release it in your time of prayer and talking to God. Moses had continuous conversation with the Lord, even when at times, he failed to carry out what was told of him to do (Numbers 20:2–11).

Even when he felt inadequate in going in the name of *I am*, he wanted someone to speak for him (Exodus 4:10–17). Even when he became angry with the people, he was delivering!

The change is so you are able to deal with every enemy, the real one and the ones you perceive on your own. Allowing yourself to be pushed to points of anger will always result in you losing out and turning around to repent because of not keeping what was put in your hands to do by God.

Watch and Pray

Jesus puts it best in *Matthew 26:41*.

Tempted to what? Handel things yourself and not allowing God in or doing it his way? Not following the instruction he gave you? Retaliate instead of allowing God to avenge you. Quit verses going the whole way through.

Temptation comes in many ways even Peter was a witness to this after walking with Jesus seeing the miracles, yet he failed (Matthew 26:42). The *temptation* came at a vulnerable time in his life (Matthew 26:75).

The real enemy is anything that stands in the way of God's greatness in you or your life. The growth will and purpose that he has, and the gaining of what is needed to do what you must!

End of chapter 4.

Review Exercise

My checklist for change

List five areas of change.

1.
2.
3.
4.
5.

List five enemies in the cross of change.

1.
2.
3.
4.
5.

Chapter 5

THE CHALLENGE
TIME TO DEFEND AND COLLECT THE REWARD!
WINNERS TAKE ALL

There are benefits to completing something, as well as the reward that follows. Maybe it is for freedom or the freedom of someone else. Maybe it is for rights, even the rights of your own! But taking a challenge is a notable thing to do when what you are fighting or standing for is of value and importance.

We see Moses's challenge cost him everything. He had to once again leave from where he was and travel, but this time, he knew, and he came into agreement with it and with God. He made himself ready to come toe to toe with the challenge of being a deliverer. God cleared his path, instructed him, told him of the outcome (not every detail) but assured him victory according to his promise to his people.

Now the test to completion was at hand. What was the battle strategy? What was his weapon? What was his recourse to the resistance that he would encounter?

God uses what's in Moses's hand to do the miraculous through (Exodus 4:2).

He will never send you to fight without armor and a weapon (Ephesians 6:10–13).

Moses's battle was with Pharaoh, a physical man, but its true intent was *spiritual.* He didn't believe in the God of the Hebrews, nor would he obey any commands, so there was a fight to contend with, and the fight was really with God!

This is true for everyone. There is a battle every day in the kingdom of darkness against the kingdom of light. The challenge is to win the soul of mankind. God has made the provision through Christ that every person can choose life over death, light over darkness, and have the *spiritual weapons* at hand. Not only are they *spiritually* a prayer away but through the authority given you as *sons and daughters,* children/offspring of the most high God, you have the right to use what has been made available, which is the word of God. The power of God and the presence of God in that will prevail against any obstacle, opponent, enemy, or foe that would ever stand in the way of a defining moment of victory in your life! (2 Corinthians 10). *Yes,* it is mighty and spiritual to the pulling down of strongholds that are present, that persist, and that are in the hearts, minds, and souls of people who oppose you and God on a daily basis.

Are you a winner? Do you see yourself a winner? Do you see yourself walking into your promised land, the thing you have been chosen by God to receive, your spiritual inheritance, your earthly portion?

Have you counted up the cost to take the stand knowing you may fold or you may fail? Well, rest assured that in accepting to go in the name of the Lord to do anything, you wouldn't go alone. Make sure it's his call and his equipment that you wear, for the attack will not just be on your *person* (though a physical attack may occur), but the emotional, intellectual, and spiritual one will be set to distort, limit, block, or even knock you right off the horse in which you will ride on.

Check your heart at the door as you go! Take no prisoners and set no bars *but* leave room for your God to unfold the mystery of himself as you have come to grips with any doubt or *question* that you *know who you are,* and it's settled.

You have answered the *call.* Even to your *true identity*, you have set out on *the quest*, and you are *up for the journey* because you've *changed* and have *dealt with the real enemy.*

What is left? Nothing but to see it all the way through, to see the salvation of the Lord for yourself and many, for after the *challenge is the victory!*

God is taking what looked like a mistake, calamity, and chaos and turned it, turning it for you and, yes, someone else. They are waiting for you, your entrance into that city town or region, waiting for the battle cry and not the continued cry of their heart out to God for help, waiting on the prayer strategy that is yet to be launched said or written, waiting on the sound of *true worship* to come forth and go throughout the world.

Yes, they are waiting for you and you and you and *you*!

For your feet to hit the ground, running to the battle for their lives to be won, for even the ones who don't yet know they need you. God is sending you to the front to lead, and in leading, you become a leader. Where? To God! To the safety of his arms, the safe place, his presence, the shelter of his house and provision.

God's making a way to be known to man. We see it written in Scripture. He has revealed himself in many ways, ways that cannot be denied that there is a *supreme being* that connects, communicates, and wants to be made known. Why? That in the midst of life's tragedies, there is hope. That life on earth is not all, and that it's not worthless. It is a gift of God! That there is peace, there is healing, there is hope in the unseen, but yet very visible God.

That is important, as well as beneficial to take the time to listen to the sent ones God has *chosen to speak for him* so that he can then talk to them directly as he always planned since the beginning of the creation of time (Genesis 2:15–17, Genesis 3:8–9).

As Moses, God's man, the messenger, prophet, mouthpiece of the Lord and those who God is still sending to this day, the challenge brings on new things and new avenues to look at and to consider.

How do we escape? How do we get the people out of their bondage? How do we complete the mission and become victorious? Remember God sent you out as a mailman to deliver something into the hands of the recipients. It is never your place or call to take part in the response of the individual. Do not take it personally but of importance that you succeed in your part. We talked about temptation. Don't allow it to cause you to abort because of the people, even the ones you are sent to free. There is no prize or reward in a job that is not well-done. It can take off, then be a misfire that will leave you more broken than when you started.

Ask (Jonah 1:3), though it may be frustrating to rescue or warn people who at times may not want to be, or you think God will forgive them, so why bother to say anything. "The message *Prophet Jonah* carried" was to tell them to *repent*. Do it any way! Don't let anything get the best of you that you become the worst of you. God has instilled too much in you that you should let him down or for you to sit down or back down. Trust that the challenge is not only for the victory of others but yours too!

As we look at Moses life, we see how he displeased God by not following what he said. We see being angry can cause sin (Ephesians 4:26). He was weary with the people he was sent to (Numbers 20:7). God said, "Speak to the rock." What did Moses do? He *smote*/hit the rock. Apparently, an offense.

He was challenged to obey verses, respond in anger and self-effort in dealing with a people who consistently complained, keeping him at a place of defending them to the Lord and the Lord to them, and carrying out the plan without feelings of being pulled in the middle is a hard task and a challenge to anyone who carries such a burden, *leadership*.

He didn't go into the Promised Land. He had seen it but didn't enter *in*. Was that sufficient? Was that what a winner would want or look like (Deuteronomy 34:1–7)?

You be the judge. These things are written for our learning (Romans 15:4) so we can see God in how he deals with his servants. Those who choose to follow him, he holds them to a higher place and Stanford of life. Why? Because you are chosen for it! Yes, you have free will, but ultimately you have the final say. If you will carry out to the letter or, as the flesh/human side of man, be weak and falter in fulfilling to the end, you come far and even to the end but not as the winner that take's *all.*

The challenge can be viewed as a burden at times, such a burden to carry and such a burden to bear.

To listen closely to the Lord, his voice, his instructions, and his word can determine if you pass or fail. Why? Because it is important!

God's not rushing things or telling you *all,* but having a method and reason for what he says and why is as important as what was laid out in the beginning of Moses's journey like yours and mine!

The ultimate challenge of all was *God* sending his *Son* to ransom the world back to himself!

There was no failure in it at all, and there, we see there was no room for human error. God knowing that the blood of bulls and goats could never take away the consciousness of *sin* from mankind, he needed a body to come down and do what could never be done in the flesh without spirit (his) living, breathing, existing, and dwelling on the inside (Hebrews 9:11–28).

Jesus the Great Contender

Who? Yes, Jesus! Living on the inside, Holy Spirit leading the way, writing the law of God on the tablets of your heart that you will always have direction in what to do and how to do it.

Jeremiah 31:33 prophesied of *Jesus* and how he would be the very writing of God in our lives, living out daily through what he did by way of his birth, life, death, burial, and resurrection. He would become the high priest passed into the heavens, making intersession for us before God (Hebrews 4:14–16). That his grace and mercy will be in and over our lives that we can carry on and carry out the call of God in doing his business. We could win! We would win!

Jesus took it all on his journey and quest into the world. He was despised and rejected of men (Isaiah 53:5). He took on human flesh, yet he was without sin (Romans 8:3). He whipped the flesh and all its works *in his flesh* so we too could have power in over and through it by him.

In order to contend, there must be opposition, an adversary lurking, opposing, and striving to pull you in the opposite direction that you should go. Always accusing and diluting minds that aren't sure or fixed to follow God or trust that whatever the path, it will be well with their soul. These are some of the things a contender will encounter, the hissing of the tongue of the enemy, whispering lies, speaking negativity to you as to how can you make it. You're not good enough, you're not strong enough, and you're not bold enough. Don't take off your gloves but *fight, fight, fight!* Even as Paul the Apostle told Timothy, fight the "good fight of faith" (1 Timothy 6:12).

That's where most of the battle takes place if not in your mind by way of your thoughts, in your heart by way of your feelings, then it trickles down to your actions. Then he hits you with condemnation that comes when you have done wrong, maybe gone astray, and you know you have failed God.

God says, "Get up! In your faith, confess and repent. I will forgive you, mean it from your heart, and I will make you free from the inside out!" (1 John 1:9).

You can win, and you can take all he has for you in this life and that to come.

As a winner, you want to *take all, all* of the instructions of God, *all* of the counsel of God, *all* of the wisdom of God, and all of the power and spirit of God to win!

He has it laid out for everyone who contends to the end, those who will run the race and finish the course (2 Timothy 4:7–8).

Even if the end is not what you hoped it to be. Don't let it be less because of your own doing. "Repent quickly." What Moses didn't have in his *time frame* was the dispensation of *God's grace*! Jesus had not come yet.

He didn't miss out on God's place of rest for his soul, but the luxuries of this world. Remember he had a lavished life in Egypt that he gave up to be with the people of God. Scripture tells us in *Psalm 84:10–11. This rang true for Moses.*

Matthew 17:1–12 shows us how Jesus at the Mount of Transfiguration had a conversation with Moses and Elijah.

That assures us that God does not disregard his children. They did not turn their backs on God though they failed to some extent and in some way. God used them as instruments in the earth in the saving of people's lives, cities, nations, just as he planned to use *his Son*. Since before the foundation of the world, he knew man would need a *savior*, and those in whom would walk the paths that led to *Jesus Christ*'s saving grace! The place where man meets God, a loving Father, a gracious friend.

To

- *those who will believe in and on him,*
- *those who will accept him,*
- *those who will follow him, and*
- *those who will obey him.*

In John 1:17, it let us know that Moses laid out the law of God in his call and walk with God and Jesus. Grace and truth make the way for it to be possible being born again of the Spirit and not relying on what causes man to fail, their own strength! Jesus paid it all, all to him we owe (John 19:30). He finished strong for all to see and receive forgiveness of sins through grace! He died that life can be given.

Question?

Are you ready for your Exodus? Your exit from one place to another.

A place of bondage and restraint to a new entry place of freedom and grace.

Are you the one who will take it all the way to victory?

Will you look failure in the eyes and say you cannot hold me? I have an advocate, the man, Christ Jesus, who saves and delivers! (1 John 2:1).

Will you hold fast to God's word for your life as though it is your last?

And will you be the instrument in which God chooses to use to save others and bring people to him?

Questions, questions, questions will always arise and be something the mind must grasp.

The question? Will you sit still long enough to get the answers? And will you put them into an action that will produce the results that are the answers for *yourself*, *others*, and those who are coming after you.

The battle is always for your *faith* whether you are new in the faith, just being called to the faith, or walking in faith for a long time.

Endurance is key in your going the distance and your standing in *faith*! Getting a glimpse of yourself and God is an intended purpose of the book, *The Moses Experience*! To see the God who created, called, and chose you in a way you may not have seen him or yourself or have even considered.

The awesome challenge is that you take it and take it all the way, yes, to the end. Whatever the call or whatever the place you may find yourself in life, there is an end, even if it's to start and have another beginning, a deeper level or a closer walk, a fresh wind to carry you on with a perspective that is infallible and unshakable. Be the winner and take all. Don't be fooled that the ending is not the picture that should be painted. God has a way that is mighty, sweet, and what looks like failure or defeat can be an end for *the* new beginning. Just trust God, stay with him, and most of *all*, obey him. If in doubt, *wait*. Wait until it is clear. Don't be moved by anything or anyone except *God*. He will reveal himself. We see that in the *Life of Moses*. He will speak, he will show you, and he will redeem you if you miss a step. Thank God, he doesn't deal with us under the Old Testament law but has given us *salvation* because of *Jesus Christ*! Grace and truth through faith in what he did on the cross. That we continue to fail or to sin, no! Romans 6:1–18, get this in your heart, get this in your mind, and *get this in your spirit*, so *you* can get up (if you've fallen) in anyway shape or form, even to believe and learn. Let the spirit of the Lord bring forth the *fruits of Holy Spirit* of God in you and in your life (Galatians 5:22–23).

> *You can do all things through Jesus Christ.* (Philippians 4:13)

And be able to say, "*It is finished!*" whether it's a test, a quest, a mission, a journey, an *assignment*, or even a trick, *you* will be *victorious* because you did not *give up!*

In conclusion of this chapter, *review and renew.*

When change is needed and there is a challenge to be succeeded, the push and energy that will get you started and going must be a day-to-day regime for any battle and for all victories! Let's look at some of the things we talked about by way of *reviewing*, and then let's take it to a place of *renewing* them. What? Your...

Mind	Body	Spirit
1. Attitude	1. Physical part of *you*	1. Be born again
2. Thoughts	2. Disciple yourself	2. Have the mind of Christ
3. Outlook	3. Submit yourself	3. Submit your spirit

Review these areas often, sometimes *daily*, then be *renewed* that you can be on track and have the peace, love, hope, and joy of the Lord that belongs to you (Romans 12:2).

This will help in accomplishing end results that will be best.

Master skills in transitioning yourself from one state of being, learning, and understanding to application. Congratulations! You are right where you should be. Just look at this as an exercise to establish that you are on the right path and remember to take others along with you. "If they are willing," always *pray*. It may not be their *time*, or you may not be the *one* who is assigned to get them there.

In closing

Throughout the pages are some examples laid out also in reference to scriptures. If you keep check on *yourself* what you think, your attitude, and your body under subjection to God's Holy Spirit, you will be able to go the distance and accomplish what you are sent to do, led to called to, and chosen for, and your own personal desire, not only that of salvation but will assist you in the things that you will face by defeating it (Galatians 5).

Be a *finisher* as Jesus Christ because God the Father has made it possible to obtain!

And enter into the promise place of your *rest*, *blessing*, *spiritual growth*, *maturity*, *leadership*, and *good example.*

That you will hear the words of the Lord say to *you*, "Well done, my good and faithful servant."

> *God is a re-warder of them that trust and obey!* (Matthew 25:14–26)

> *But without faith it is impossible to please him: for he that cometh to God must believe that he is, and that he is a rewarder of them that diligently seek him.* (Hebrews 11:6)

BATTLE FOR MY FAITH

I WILL WALK IN THE LIGHT OF THE SUN
WHEN THE STORMS OF LIFE STOP RAGING AND THE BATTLE IS DONE
THE WARMTH OF ITS RAYS WILL SHINE UPON MY FACE
I AM NOW BEING LIFTED FOR I AM SAVED BY HIS GRACE
THE CLOUDS ARE MOVING STEADILY BY
I SEE THE SUN BEGINNING TO SHINE
AS IT RISES FROM BENEATH THE CLOUDS AND MOVES HASTILY ON
ITS SHINING NOW FOR ME TO SEE
NO MORE TEARS OF SORROW
NOW TEARS OF JOY WILL OVERTAKE ME
FOR I WILL WALK IN THE LIGHT OF THE SUN
THE BATTLE IS OVER AND THE VICTORY IS WON

About the Author

Born and raised in Pennsylvania, while growing up in the church was a plus, when trouble hits, knowing where to go and where to turn made the difference and outcome for many of life's experiences and situations.

From as early as a baby, I was taught firsthand from my mother, the late Evangelist Ella K. Johnson, who represented what the realness of God meant, his word and his love, and at that time also from my church family, Victory Temple Original Church of God, where the late Rev. Dr. Dorothy M. Lewis Jones, pastor and founder, is one of the first African American women in the city of Pittsburgh recognized in this light by Mayor "Richard Caliguiri," who commemorated this by noting it down in history as such.

Through those powerful moments, times, and services, I witnessed the salvation of many souls being saved, lives of people had changed, and being told, I realized God had a plan for me too. It caused me to look at each person in the Bible and relate to them in some way.

When the Moses experience was placed on my heart to write about and share with people, I was moved with compassion in understanding God was really talking to me first. So I was humbled in the middle of writing. Many times, I had to *stop* and worship the Lord, thanking him for his loving-kindnesses to me, to the people we read about in Scripture, and to the people he will speak to through this book.

I am a Ordained Pastor/Minister with an Organization for Women & Children. "Our Sisters Keeper". A Licensed Cosmetologist & Barber Trainer. Certified in Life & Business Coaching.

CPSIA information can be obtained
at www.ICGtesting.com
Printed in the USA
BVHW031439220821
614829BV00001B/1

9 781639 038619